HOW-TO LIBRARY

TABLE OF CONTENTS

The History of Clay

Dogu figures were made in Japan beginning 16,000 years ago.

Since ancient times, people have used clay to make pottery, decorative art, and construction materials such as bricks and tiles. Clay is a type of soil found naturally in the earth. It contains **minerals** that make it easy to mold when it is mixed with water. Clay becomes firm when dried. When **fired** in an oven or **kiln**, it becomes very hard.

Some of the earliest pottery ever discovered was found in Japan. It dates back to 14,000 BCE. Other ancient societies used clay tablets for writing. These tablets are some of the first known records of written language. Workers called scribes wrote down events and stories that could be passed on from generation to generation.

In recent times, people have improved on the natural clay that was used by ancient civilizations. Ceramic clay is one kind of modern clay. It starts with a clay mineral base similar to the kind that was used in ancient times. Other raw materials are added to make it more **durable** and easier to stretch. Polymer clay is another type of clay that is commonly used today. It does not contain any natural clay minerals, but it can be molded and shaped much like natural clay can.

Ceramic clay is used to make many objects, from plates and pots to decorations.

Many Types of Clay

Colorful modeling clay is easy to find in stores, but you can also make your own at home.

Clay comes in a wide variety of colors and can be used to make an even wider variety of things. There are several types of modeling clay available in stores. They range from inexpensive clays for kids to expensive clays for creating fine art. You can also make your own clay from simple ingredients at home (*see pages 8–10*).

Reusable modeling clay does not harden. It is great for creating and re-creating endless projects. For example, animators use it to create sculptures for claymation films. Many of the projects in this book can be completed with reusable, non-hardening clay.

Clay that hardens cannot be reused once it is dry. It is a perfect choice for projects that you want to keep. You should use hardening clay for projects that you want to give as presents or display on a shelf.

There are three types of hardening clay:

- **Air-dry clay:** This clay is easy to work with. It hardens by sitting out in open air for about 24 to 48 hours.
- **Polymer clay:** Most polymer clay is hardened by baking it in a kitchen oven. Polymer clays are usually more durable than air-dry clays. Make sure there is an adult who can help you use the oven if you choose this type of clay.
- **Ceramic clay:** Ceramic clay is hardened by baking it at a very high temperature. Kitchen ovens cannot get this hot. You will need to use a kiln instead. Many schools have kilns available. Talk to your art teacher if you are interested in using ceramic clay.

Clay Recipes

You can make your own clay using common household ingredients. Below are a few different clay recipes.

Flour and Salt Clay Recipe

This clay can be reused if you store it in the refrigerator. It does not last as long as store-bought, non-hardening clays, though. It can also be baked if you want to harden it.

Materials

- 4 cups flour
- 1 cup salt
- 1½ cups water
- Food coloring (optional)

Steps

1. Mix the flour, salt, and water together in a large bowl.
2. Add a few drops of food coloring if you want to make colored clay.
3. If you are not using the clay right away, store it in a sealed plastic bag in the refrigerator. Squeeze as much air as possible out of the bag before sealing it. This will stop the clay from drying out.
4. Bake your finished art project in an oven at 350°F (177°C) for 1 hour to harden it. Cool the baked clay on a wire rack before handling or painting it.

Simple Air-Dry Cornstarch Clay

This easy-to-make clay can be hardened by letting it sit in open air for 24 to 48 hours.

Materials

- 1 cup water
- 1½ cups table salt
- Saucepan
- 1 cup cornstarch
- Food coloring (optional)

Steps

1. Combine the water and table salt in the saucepan.
2. Bring the water to a boil while stirring to dissolve the salt. Ask an adult to help you use the stove.
3. Once the salt is dissolved, remove the saucepan from the heat and quickly add the cornstarch. Stir until the mixture is sticky and stiff.
4. Stir in a few drops of food coloring if you want to make colored clay.
5. If you are not using the clay right away, store it in a sealed plastic bag in the refrigerator. Squeeze as much air as possible out of the bag before sealing it.

Homemade Air-Dry Polymer Clay

Not all types of polymer clay need to be baked in the oven. Create your own homemade air-dry polymer clay with this simple recipe.

Materials

- ¾ cup white glue
- 1 cup cornstarch
- Nonstick pot
- Wooden spoon
- 2 tablespoons mineral oil plus extra for removing it from the pot
- 1 tablespoon lemon juice
- Food coloring (optional)

Steps

1. Mix the glue and cornstarch together in the nonstick pot, using the wooden spoon. Add the mineral oil and lemon juice. Blend well.
2. Ask an adult to help to cook the mixture over low heat. Stir constantly until the mixture resembles mashed potatoes.
3. Remove the pot from the heat. When the clay is cool enough to touch, but still hot, add a small amount of mineral oil around the top of the clay. Use your hands to remove the clay from the pot. Ask an adult to help you.
4. **Knead** the clay until it is smooth. It is best to do this while the clay is still as hot as you can handle. Knead in a few drops of food coloring if you want to make colored clay.
5. If you are not using the clay right away, store it in a sealed plastic bag in the refrigerator. Squeeze as much air as possible out of the bag before sealing it.

Gather Materials

Once you have purchased or made your clay, you can gather a variety of tools and other materials to help you mold your clay creations.

- **Clay tools** (wooden or plastic) are essential for working with clay. There are many clay tools available from craft stores. Choose the ones that look most helpful to you.
- **Toothpicks** can be used to create tiny details.
- **Acrylic paint** and **brushes** can add color to your creations.
- **Food coloring** can add more colors to your clay.
- **Feathers**, **plastic eyes**, **beads**, **pipe cleaners**, **sequins**, and **sand** can all be used as decorations for your sculptures.
- **Parchment paper** is used to protect your work surface.

Before you start working with any clay, it is important to protect your work surface. Some clay can stain a table. Always cover your work surface with parchment paper.

Next you need to condition your clay. Conditioning the clay is done by rolling and kneading it until it is **pliable** and easy to work with. You should do this before starting any of the projects in this book. Conditioned clay will not crack as you work with it.

You are now ready to create!

TIP
If you do not have the right color clay, you can always paint your project after it dries. You can also add food coloring to your clay to make it the right color. Food coloring works best if you start with white clay.

Silly Clay Portraits

Use modeling clay to give yourself a crazy new look. Make over photos of friends and family members for the perfect gift!

Materials

- Portrait photograph printed on 8½ x 11-inch (22 x 28 cm) paper
- Box for spraying
- Spray mount **adhesive**
- 8½ x 11-inch (22 x 28 cm) foam core board
- Reusable, non-hardening colored clay or air-dry clay (many different colors)

Steps

1. Place your portrait, face side down, in the box for spraying. Spray the back of your portrait with spray mount. Stick the portrait to the foam core.

2. Mold pieces of clay into hair, clothing, and accessories, and then stick them onto the photograph. You can follow the portrait exactly, or you can create wild hair and accessories.

3. Use your imagination and create a monster or alien portrait. You can turn your portrait into a clown face by adding a red nose and big red lips. Turn your portrait into a cowboy by sculpting a cowboy hat and a mustache.

4. You can create a funny feathery hat by sticking feathers into the clay.

5. Leave a portion of the portrait clear of clay so you can tell who is underneath the silly clay creation.

Crazy Clay Creatures

These crazy clay creatures make wonderful gifts. Be sure to use a clay that hardens if you plan on giving your creature to someone. The creatures make great paperweights and bookends. They can also just sit on the shelf and make someone smile.

Materials

- Green, purple, blue, or pink clay (color choice is up to you)
- Pipe cleaners for arms and legs (optional)
- Googly eyes or beads
- Tools, toothpicks
- Feathers or sequins

Steps

1. Pick any color of clay and roll balls to make the head and body of your creature. Some creatures may only need one ball. It is up to you. Be creative.
2. Use pipe cleaners to create arms and legs. You can also build arms and legs using more clay.
3. Add big red lips or simply form a mouth on the face of your creature.

4. Use clay to form horns and add them to your creature's head.

5. You can attach plastic googly eyes or beads to make eyes.

6. Use a toothpick or clay tools to help shape small details.

7. Add feathers to make your creature birdlike. Use sequins to add shiny spots.

8. Below are several different ideas you can try. You can create your own crazy creature as well.

9. Dry or bake your creation according to the instructions on the clay package.

TIP
If you are using clay that needs to be baked, do not use plastic eyes or beads. Feathers and pipe cleaners are not a good choice either. They will melt or burn in the oven. If you would like to use these items, choose an air-dry or non-hardening clay.

Prickly Porcupine

This pointy new friend has a body made of clay, and quills made from toothpicks.

Materials
- Brown or black clay
- Small piece of pink clay
- Googly eyes or beads
- Toothpicks
- Sculpting tools

Steps
1. Pinch off a golf-ball-size piece from the brown or black clay and roll it into a ball.
2. Roll one end of the ball so it forms a point. Add a small piece of pink clay at the end of the point to give your porcupine a nose.

3. Pinch off four marble-size pieces from your brown or black clay. Roll them into balls. These are your porcupine's feet. Place them on the bottom of the larger ball.

4. Add eyes with beads or googly eyes.

5. Poke the toothpicks into your porcupine's body to form the quills.

6. Dry or bake your creation according to the instructions on the clay package. If you are using clay that needs to be baked, do not use plastic items. They will melt in the oven. Wooden toothpicks and beads work best in the oven.

7. Be careful picking up your porcupine. He is prickly!

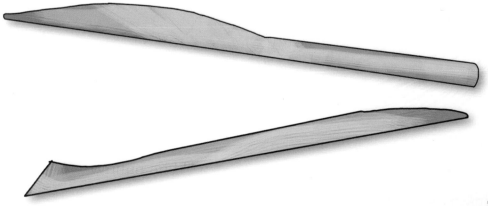

Proud Peacock

Create a fun and colorful peacock with real feathers!

Materials

- Air-dry or non-hardening blue or teal clay
- 2 yellow pipe cleaners
- 1 blue pipe cleaner
- Googly eyes
- Green sequins
- Blue, green, purple, and teal feathers
- Glue

Steps

1. Pinch off a golf-ball-size piece from the blue or teal clay and roll it into a ball. To form the body pinch the ball into a kidney bean shape.
2. Cut one of the yellow pipe cleaners into two 5-inch (13 cm) sections. Fold each section into feet as shown.
3. Poke the feet into the bottom of the clay ball.

4. Cut a 5-inch (13 cm) section of blue pipe cleaner and roll the top as shown, to make the peacock's head.
5. Cut a 1-inch (2.5 cm) section from the other yellow pipe cleaner. Fold it in half and secure it to the peacock's head for the beak.
6. Glue a googly eye on each side of the peacock's head.
7. Poke the peacock's head into place on the clay body.
8. Glue sequins to the front chest of your peacock.
9. Add your peacock's tail feathers.

TIP
What other kinds of birds can you make out of clay? Use a sketchbook to draw your ideas. This will help you plan what materials you will need.

Clay Food

Clay food can be fun to play with, but you don't want to eat it! You can make cupcakes, hamburgers, hot dogs, sushi, cookies, doughnuts, or pizza. The possibilities are endless. Make your food out of a polymer clay that hardens in the oven for a creation you can play with for a long time.

Materials for Hamburger

- Clay for bun (tan)
- Sesame seeds (white)
- Toothpicks
- Burger (brown)
- Cheese (yellow)
- Clay tools
- Lettuce (green)
- Tomato (red)

Steps

1. Pinch off a golf-ball-size piece from the tan clay to make the bun. Roll it into a ball and cut it in half. Flatten each half into a bun shape.

2. Use tiny pieces of white clay to form sesame seeds. Stick the seeds to the top side of the bun. Use a toothpick to help place and stick them if they are too small for your fingers to handle.

3. Use the brown clay to form a hamburger patty that fits on the bun. Place it on top of the bottom bun half.

4. Make cheese out of the yellow clay. Cut it with your clay tool to make it square. Place it on your hamburger.

5. Make lettuce from the green clay. Roll the clay into a ball and flatten it. Curl the edges up and down to create the edges of the lettuce. Place it on top of the cheese.

6. Make a tomato slice from the red clay. Roll the red clay into a ball, and then flatten it into a circle. Roll the edge of the circle along the table to flatten the edges of the tomato. Place the tomato slice on top of the lettuce.

7. Place the top of the bun on top of the tomato.

8. Dry your sculpture according to the directions on the package.

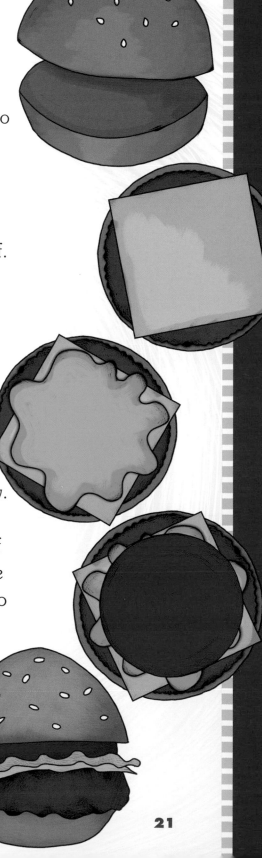

Gumball Machine

Materials

- Multicolored clay
- Old newspapers
- Mini $1\frac{3}{4}$-inch (4.5 cm) terra-cotta pot
- Red acrylic paint
- Paintbrush and water
- Clear plastic Christmas tree ornament

Steps

1. Pinch off a gumball-size piece from any color of clay and roll it into a ball. It should be small enough to fit through the top opening of your Christmas tree ornament.
2. Repeat step one to make 30 small gumballs in a variety of colors.
3. Dry the gumballs according to the directions on the package.
4. While the gumballs are drying, spread newspapers on your work surface.
5. Paint the terra-cotta pot red and let it dry.

6. Once the gumballs are dried and cooled, remove the top of the ornament. Drop the balls into the ornament. Once the balls are all inside, place the top back on the ornament.

7. Turn the ornament upside down and set it in the terra-cotta pot.

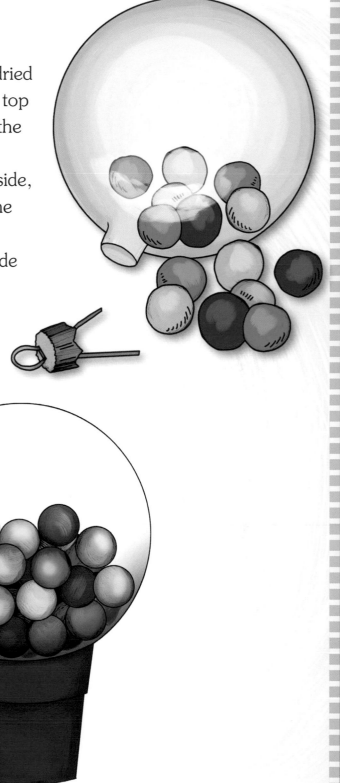

Rose Vase

This vase is so beautiful that you will not even need to put flowers in it. You can if you want to, though!

Materials

- Red, pink, or yellow air-dry clay for flowers
- Clay tool
- Green air-dry clay for leaves
- Glass vase or jar

Steps

1. Pinch off a marble-size piece from your flower-colored clay and roll it into a ball. Repeat until you have 10 small balls. These will become your flower petals.
2. Flatten the balls into circles. Do not make them too thin or they will rip.
3. Choose the smallest circle and roll it into a spiral. This will become the center of your rose.
4. Choose another clay circle and wrap it around the spiral you just created. Gently pinch the petals together at the bottom. The circle may not wrap all the way around the spiral.

5. Pick up another clay circle and place it where the last circle ended. Start wrapping it around the spiral and the previous petal. Gently push down on the last two clay circles so they start to roll down and form the top curl of the petal.

6. Repeat step five until all of your clay circles have been used.

7. Gently pinch the bottom of the flower together. Use your clay tool to cut the excess clay away from the bottom of the rose so it has a flat bottom.

8. Pinch off a marble-size piece from the green clay and roll it into a ball.

9. Flatten the ball into a circle as you did for the flower petals.

10. Use your clay tool to cut the shape of a leaf out of the circle.

11. Stick the clay leaf and flower to the side of your vase.

12. Repeat steps 1 through 11 to make an entire ring of roses around the top of your vase. You can also add flowers to the bottom of the vase if you would like to.

13. Allow the vase to sit until it is completely dry (about 24 to 48 hours) before using it.

Mini Sandcastle

You don't need to visit the beach to make this sandcastle. And you don't have to worry about it being knocked down by waves!

Materials

- Brown or tan air-dry or non-hardening clay
- Clay tools
- Sand
- Paper plate
- Scissors
- Colored paper
- Glue
- Toothpicks
- Seashells

Steps

1. Pinch off a gumball-size piece of tan or brown clay. Form it into a cube. This will be the center building in your castle.

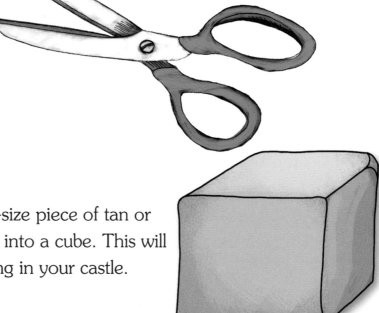

2. Pinch off another gumball-size piece of clay and roll it into a cylinder. Stick the cylinder to one corner of the cube. Make sure it is securely attached. This will be one of the castle towers.

3. Repeat step two to make three more towers, one for each corner of the cube.

4. Use your clay tools to carve a door and windows into your castle. You can carve as many additional details as you would like.

5. Put the sand on your paper plate. Gently roll your castle in the sand. You may need to use your fingers to get the sand to stick on some parts of the sculpture.

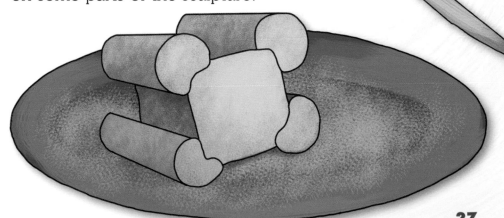

6. Use your scissors to cut four small paper diamonds from the colored paper. These four diamonds will become flags for the towers.

7. Fold each of the diamonds in half to create a crease. Add glue to one side of each crease.

8. Place a toothpick along a crease and fold the paper around the toothpick to stick the two sides together. Do this to each of the folded diamonds.

9. Attach your flags to the towers.

10. Add seashells if you would like to further decorate your castle.

Other Creative Clay Ideas

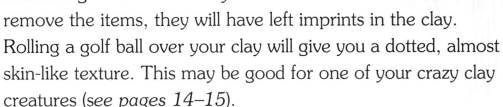

As you may have discovered, the things you can make with clay are endless. So are the methods you can use to decorate your sculptures. For example, you can press or roll items on your clay to create interesting textures. When you remove the items, they will have left imprints in the clay. Rolling a golf ball over your clay will give you a dotted, almost skin-like texture. This may be good for one of your crazy clay creatures (see pages 14–15).

You can wrap clay around the end of a pencil and create a decoration that everyone in class will want. You can make small beads or large pots. What other creations can you think of?

Carry a sketchbook with you to draw your ideas. Sketching your ideas helps you plan how to create new sculptures. You can also make lists of materials you will need to create your new sculptures. You never know when you'll come up with a great new idea!

Glossary

adhesive (ad-HEE-siv) a substance, such as glue, that makes things stick together

durable (DUR-uh-buhl) tough and lasting for a long time

fired (FYE-urd) baked at a high temperature in a kiln

kiln (KILN) a very hot oven used to bake or dry bricks, pottery, or other objects made of clay

knead (NEED) to press, fold, and stretch dough with your hands to make it smooth

minerals (MIN-ur-uhlz) solid substances found in the earth that do not come from animals or plants

pliable (PLYE-uh-buhl) easily bent or shaped

For More Information

Books

Henry, Sally. *Clay Modeling*. New York: PowerKids Press, 2009.

Storey, Rita. *Clay*. North Mankato, MN: Smart Apple Media, 2008

Web Sites

How Stuff Works—Clay Crafts for Kids

http://lifestyle.howstuffworks.com/crafts/other-arts-crafts/clay-crafts.htm

Check out this Web site for other homemade clay recipes and craft ideas.

Spoonful—Crafts for Kids to Make

http://spoonful.com/family-fun/clay-crafts

If you're looking for more ideas, just visit this site for lots more projects to try.

Index

About the Author

Kathleen Petelinsek is a children's book illustrator, writer, and designer. As a child, she spent her summers drawing and painting. She still loves to do the same today, but now all her work is done on the computer. When she isn't working on her computer, she can be found outside swimming, biking, running, or playing in the snow of southern Minnesota.